ALLAN MORRISON is a prolific autho[r...]
include *Haud Ma Chips, Ah've Drapped the Wean!*, *Should've Gone tae Specsavers, Ref!* and *Last Tram tae Auchenshuggle!* These books all combine three of his passions: humour, nostalgia and Glasgow. His media appearances include *The One Show* and *The Fred MacAulay Show.*

He is involved in charity work, after-dinner speaking and is a member of his local Rotary club. Allan enjoys hill-walking, sport and travel. He and his wife live the West of Scotland and he is the proud grandfather of four grandchildren.

'Goanae No Dae That!'

The best of the best of those cracking Scottish sayings!

ALLAN MORRISON

with illustrations by
BOB DEWAR

Luath Press Limited
EDINBURGH
www.luath.co.uk

First published 2014
Reprinted 2015
Reprinted 2016
Reprinted 2017

ISBN: 978-1-910021-57-6

The paper used in this book is recyclable. It is made from
low chlorine pulps produced in a low energy, low emissions manner
from renewable forests.

Printed and bound by
CPI Antony Rowe, Chippenham

Typeset in Quadraat and MetaPlus
by 3btype.com

Contents

Introduction

Some people say that when God made Scotland he was just showing off, for not only did he give us a beautiful land to live in, he also left us with some cracking sayings, phrases, words and havers with which to communicate. Most comprise a homely form of common sense, perhaps helping to shape our lives.

Scottish sayings hit the spot right away in a cheeky sort of way, indicating the feelings and observations of the speaker. Most of the sayings in this book are contemporary, some a little older but all are relevant to today's society. Many will challenge the reader and make them think on the implications behind the saying. Others were clearly created to assist you through life, give you practical advice and keep you on the straight and narrow. Some advise on character, happiness, and keep you vigilant. Quite a few were no doubt created by individuals who had learned the hard way by their mistakes and wanted to pass on a warning to others.

All of the Scottish sayings are followed by a translation... if you really need it. I trust you will laugh, reflect and enjoy this wonderful set of the best of the best of Scottish sayings.

As one of the sayings states, 'Castles fa' doon but wise words stay.' I hope this is indeed the case with this book.

Acknowledgements

My thanks go to Andrew Pearson and Archie Wilson for their significant contribution.

Acknowledgement

Appearance

'Ye've a dial oan ye like a well-smacked erse.'
You are not looking your best today.

'She's goat a set o' new wallies.'
She has a new set of false teeth.

'Ye look like wan o'clock half struck.'
You are only half awake.

'Yer herr's mingin', hingin' an' clingin'.'
What kind of state is your hair in?

'GOANAE NO DAE THAT!'

'A pot lid wid suit a bonnie wean.'
Pretty people can just about wear anything.

'Ye look like a deserter oot a kirkyard.'
You look half-dead.

'Ye look like the cat's elbow.'
You're too thin.

'Yer herr looks like straw hingin' oot a midden.'
You do not appear to have brushed your hair.

'Och, freckles are jist God's kisses.'
There is nothing to worry about.

'Ye look like somethin' the cat dragged in.'
You are unkempt.

'There's no' twa pun o' her hingin' the same way.'
She is too fat.

'Ye've goat a face like cake left oot in the rain.'
Your face is getting somewhat worn.

'He's goat some coupon oan him.'
He has an unusual face.

'Yer hair is cut tae the knuckle.'
Your hair is very short.

'Ye could fry twa eggs oan that hair.'
Your hair is greasy.

'Yer dial's full o' plooks.'
You have spots on your face.

'He's a tattie-lugged loon.'
That boy has big ears.

'That wan is lang-nebbit.'
He is a nosy, prying individual.

Blethering

'Aye, right!'
I don't totally believe you.

'Yer doin' ma heid in!'
Stop talking!

'Good job it's no' summer else yer tongue wid be burnt.'
You talk too much.

'Wheesht yer puss.'
Be quiet.

'Haud yer wheesht.'
Be quiet.

'That wan's the talk o' the steamie.'
Everyone is talking about them.

'Yer aw bum an' parsley.'
You're big-headed.

'A lie is half-way roon Scotland afore the truth has its boots oan.'
Be careful what you say.

'Wan who gossips hae nae freens tae speak o'.'
People do not like others who pass on personal information.

'Ah've a guid Scotch tongue in ma heid.'
I can communicate as well as anybody.

'That's Jock's news.'
I've heard that already.

'Wur tearin' the tartan.'
We are having a good blether.

'GOANAE NO DAE THAT!'

**'Wur youse vaccinated wi'
a gramophone needle?'**
You are forever talking.

'Hit that wi' a tattie.'
That is quite posh.

'Yon's twa-faced an' nane of them's pretty.'
They are totally untrustworthy.

'Ah wis fair black affronted.'
I was so embarrassed.

'Yer heid's full o' mince.'
You are talking nonsense.

'Blether aw, say nought.'
People who talk a lot rarely say anything of importance.

'Ah'm fair scunnered.'
I am fed up.

'That wan's in everything but the Co-operative windae.'
They are in a lot of organisations.

'Look at the ding o' that wan.'

They are all dressed up giving the impression they have a high opinion of themselves.

'Aye, ye'll go. An' a tuppenny haepenny stamp will no' bring ye back.'

You are going whether you like it or not.

'Ah'm fair dumfoonert.'

I'm confused.

'Birds an' blethers baith fly.'

Stories quickly get around.

'It's a braw, bricht moonlicht nicht the nicht.'
Yes, I am Scottish.

'That wan wid breastfeed her wean through the school railings.'
She spoils her children.

'Yer heid's in a fankle.'
You seem confused

Clothes

'It's like twa duck eggs in a hankie.'

Your bottom is rather pronounced in that outfit.

'It wis sewn wi' a hot needle in a burnin' haun.'
It is poorly made.

'Is the cat deid?'
Your trousers are somewhat short.

'That maks ye look like a tattiebogle.'
You look like a scarecrow in that outfit.

'Ur ye goin' tae the hoor's ball?'
Your clothes are too revealing.

'Ye've feet like a catch o' kippers.'
Your feet are quite large.

'Yon couldna think withoot his bunnet.'
You never see him without headware.

'Looks like a half-eaten fleabag.'
He is poorly dressed.

'Get yer genzie oan.'
Put on your navy jersey.

Death

'Folks die, but the toon clock still chimes.'
Life goes on.

'They've goat the look o' wet clay
aboot them.'
I think they are dying.

'Their heid's nae sair that did it.'
Whoever did this must have died long ago.

'Ah've freens in baith places.'
Some of my friends have gone to Heaven
and some to Hell.

'GOANAE NO DAE THAT!'

'Death is the cost fur livin'.'
We pay for living by having to die.

'It's no' the ramblin' cart that fa's first ower the brae.'
It's not always the person you think will die first who does.

'He jist woke up deid.'
He died in his sleep.

'Better late than early wi' the angels.'
Take your time.

'Death's a payment each man maun mak.'
Death comes to everyone.

'Better tae bust oot than rust oot.'
Get the best out of life before you go.

'Thon's death oan a pirn stick.'
They look as though they do not have long to go.

'If yer no afraid tae die ye'll only die the wance.'
Live for today and forget the future.

Drink

'Mony a pub has artists though nane can paint.'
Some people in pubs just like to drink.

'Yer oot yer face.'
You are drunk.

'He's oan the bevvy.'
He likes quite a lot of drink.

'Ah've a fair drooth oan me.'
I am thirsty.

'Naebuddy cares aboot yer accent as long as yer scotch is guid.'

Drink is important to many people.

'Some get fu' after wan drink; usually their tenth!'

Some people can drink a lot of alcohol.

'Thon's guttered.'

They are very drunk.

'Ne'er drink oan an empty pocket.'

Drinking can be expensive.

'When the dram's inside the sense is ootside.'
Alcohol can make you lose your inhibitions.

'Ah jist loved sugarelly-watter wance ah'd left it under the bed fur a week.'
I liked to drink water with liquorice in it after it has been kept in the dark for a week to mature (usually under a bed).

'Gae's a wee swally.'
Let me have a taste.

'Drams bring truth unca close.'
People lose their tact with alcohol.

Expressions

'Away an' go yer dinger.'
Go and get on with it.

'Howzit goin', big man?'
How are you?

'Yer cruisin' fur a bruisin'.'
Just watch it!

'The place wis fair hoachin'.
It was over busy.

'Ah'm knackered apart fae the soles o' ma shoes.'

I am exhausted.

'Bachelor's wives an' auld maid's bairns are aye well fed.'

You have no experience on this subject.

'Ya beauty!'

That's great.

'Help ma boab.'

I am surprised.

'This is me since yesterday.'
I have been feeling like this for a couple of days.

'Yer like a half-shut knife.'
You don't appear to be functioning well today.

'Yon's a rerr terr.'
They are a good laugh.

'Oot oan the ran dan.'
Enjoying a wild night on the town.

'Yer a right warmer.'
You are something else.

'It's better than a slap oan the dial wi' a wet haddie.'
It is better than nothing.

'Some things hae an end but a loaf has twa.'
There is always an exception to the rule.

'Yawright?'
Are you okay?'

'Goanae no dae that!'
Please refrain from doing that again.

'Takers eat well an' givers sleep well.'
Kind people tend to have an easy conscience.

'You jist open yer mooth an' let yer belly rumble.'
You say a lot of stupid things.

'Twelve herrings an' a bagpipe mak a rebellion.'
You are exaggerating.

'Skedaddle aff.'
Away you go.

'A troot in the pan is better than a salmon in the Tay.'
Better to have something than something you may never have.

'Exaggeration is jist truth that lost its temper.'
People can make outrageous statements when they are angry.

'Ma heid's fair burstin'.'
I am confused.

'Away an' pit her heid in the jawbox.'
Get lost. If necessary stick your head in the sink.

'Ye need tae dae whit ye have tae dae, afore ye can dae whit ye want tae dae.'
You need to plan ahead.

'It's awfa difficult choosin' between twa clean coos.'
They all look the same.

'Away an' tummle yer wilkies.'
Go and do something different.

'A blind man runnin' for a bus widnae notice.'
You are fine the way you are.

'It wid dae a blind man guid tae see it.'
Everyone would like this.

'Facts are chiels that winna ding.'
You cannot argue with facts.

'Yer as auld fashioned as a tea pot.'
You don't keep up with fashion trends.

'That's the baw up oan the slates.'
Now we are in trouble.

'That's the best feather in yer wing.'
That is what you are best at.

'Stick it up yer jowks.'
Put it under your jumper or jacket.

'Ye've a face oan ye like a constipated coo.'
Is something wrong with you?

'Ne'er blaw yer ain nose.'
Only let other people praise you.

'Ye cannae tak the breeks aff a Heilinman.'
You cannot take something from someone who
doesn't have it.

'Ah'm gonnae go ma dinger in a minute.'
I am just about to lose my temper.

'It's no often ah'm wrang but ah'm right again.'
I am always correct.

'Ye'll get drookit the day.'
It is raining and you'll get soaked.

'So, who stole yer scone?'
Why are you upset?

'They're aw there an' back again.'
They are sharp.

'Clerty clerty!'
Goodness me.

'GOANAE NO DAE THAT!'

'Away an' dry yer chin.'
Be quiet.

'The funny wee man wi' nae legs wull catch a hare.'
Don't be silly.

'It'll be a skoosh.'
It will be easy.

'Ye can gang faur an' fare waur.'
You could travel further than here and do worse than this.

'Of all ills, nane is best.'
It is better to have no problems.

'Whit's fur ye wull no go by ye.'
Whatever is meant for you in life you will get.

'Maybe aye an' maybe hooch aye.'
I am doubtful.

'Ye deserve a right shirrakin.'
You deserve to be told off.

'Gaun yersell!'
Keep trying.

**'That wan is as cute as a dumplin'
in a hankie.'**
They are something special.

**'Dinnae trouble trouble till trouble
troubles you.'**
Don't go looking for problems.

'Ye can aye throw stanes at yer ain Baillies.'
You are allowed to criticise officials you voted for.

'It's gey driech the day.'

It's a miserable depressing day.

'Comfort comes in auld claes.'

Friends you have had over many years are reliable.

'If ye want a freen, be a freen.'

If you want friends then take the initiative.

'It's nae loss whit a freen gets.'

If you are unsuccessful then it is consoling to know that a friend has been.

'Dae ye think ah came up the Clyde oan a bike?'
Do you think I am daft!

'Yer at it!'
You are trying to fool me.

'Och yer bahoochie.'
You are wrong.

'It isnae even worth a paper poke
wi' a twirly end.'
It is absolutely worthless.

'Yon is aw houchty-pouchty.'
They think they are high and mighty.

'It was really jist a Kelso convoy.'
I just accompanied them for a short distance.

'Ah jist love they merry dancers.'
I like looking at the aurora borealis.

Family Life

'If ye don't behave ah'll pawn ye an'
sell the ticket.'

A threat to stop you misbehaving.

'Tell Ben tae come ben. If Ben doesnae come
ben, then tell Ben I'll be ben tae bring Ben ben.'

Tell that one to get a move on or I'll come and get him.

'If ye dinnae stop greetin' ah'll gae ye somethin'
tae greet fur.'

If you don't stop crying you may well regret it.

'Behave yersell or ah'll shoot the boots aff ye.'

Behave or I will take extreme measures.

'Stop ringin' that clapper.'

Hold your tongue.

'Wan mere word oot o' you an' yer pan breid.'

Be quiet!

'Ye've jist ga'en yer face a coo's lick.'

You have merely given your face a quick wipe.

'Away an' pap peas at yer granny.'

Go away and do not annoy me. (To pap is to throw)

'Ah'll chop yer heid aff an' sew on a button.'

Behave or I will be taking some action.

'Geeza brek.'

I am running out of patience with you.

'Ye'll go wi' yer lip trimblin'.'

Regardless what you say, you will do it.

'Ah think they goat ye in a lucky bag.'

I don't really know where you came from.

'Dicht yer neb an' flee awa'.'
Wipe your nose and go.

'Nae fizzers noo.'
Do not tell me lies.

'Yer the mither o' mischief an'
no' bigger than a midge's wing.'
You are mischievous.

'Ah'll gae ye a Hawick Hug.'
I will squeeze you around the middle.

'Ye've two choices. Eat yer dinner or leave it.
But see if ye leave it, ye'll get it fur yer tea.'
Eat your dinner!

'Jist wait tae yer fether gets hame.'
You can expect some punishment when
your father arrives home.

'Ye fether's goat his ain back teeth.'
Your father is not a foolish person.

'If ah take ma haun aff yer bum
ye'll never smile again.'
If you don't behave I will need to take
some action.

'Have ye goat the best seat oan
the midden the day?'
Are you in a bad mood?

'Yer a wee stoater.'
I am proud of you.

'Ye don't need tae brush aw yer teeth.
Jist the wans ye want tae keep.'
Give your teeth a thorough clean.

'In a minute ah'll clatter ye wi' ma bunnet.'
Stop misbehaving.

'Ah'm fed up wi' the hale jing bang lot o' ye.'

I am nearing the end of my tether.

'Soup should be seen an' no' heard.'

Do not make a noise as you sup your soup.

'Aw yer gettin' is a run roon the table an' a kick at the cat.'

I'm not telling you what you will get for your next meal.

'Ah'll gae ye wan an' lend ye another.'

Do you want a smacking?

'If ye step oan a nail yer faither's in jile.'

Stop doing what you are doing.

'Ah dinnae lift ye afore ye fa'.'

I don't find any fault with you until you give me cause.

'Nae cauld joints oan the table.'

It is impolite to have your elbows on the table.

'Aye, an ye'll only get it when a coo calves a cuddie.'

You are never going to get it.

'If ye pick dandelions, ye'll pee the bed.'
Everything has consequences.

'Whit did yer last slave die o'?'
You are lazy.

'Aye, an' yer belly button is where the angels poked ye tae see if you were ready.'
Don't be daft.

If ye pick yer nose yer heid'll cave in.'
Don't pick your nose.

'Wan minute yer a peacock an'
the next yer a feather duster.'
Things change quickly.

'Hae a wee coorie-in.'
Snuggle in.

'In a minute ye'll hae yer heid in
yer hauns tae play wi'.'
Behave or else.

'Ah'll gae ye a skelpit lug!'
I'll warm your ear for you.

'Whit gangs roon comes aroon.'
Everybody gets their turn in life.

**'Close that windae.
Yer heating the hale o' Scotland.'**
You are wasting the heat in this house
that I am paying for.

'That wan's thrown a big stone at ma door.'
They've stopped talking to me.

'If ye keep whistlin' yer hair wull fa' oot.'
Stop whistling!

'As the auld cock craws, the young craw learns.'
You learn from the actions of your elders.

'Ye'll laugh oan the ither side o' yer face in a minute.'
Behave or you will be very sorry.

'Yer face looks like the far end o' a French fiddle.'
You look as though you are going to whine.

'Bairns an' fools should no' see work half done.'
Be an example to everyone.

'Ye won't be happy till yer greetin'.'
There is no pleasing you.

'Ah'll gae ye laldy!'
I will give you more than you expect!

'It's a bit shooglie.'
It is wobbling.

'Weans wi' big ears tak it aw in.'
Children hear everything that is going on.

'Hell slap it intae ye.'
It's your own fault.

'Use it up, wear it oot, mak it do or do withoot.'
Do not waste anything.

**'Tween three an' thirteen,
thran the woodie when it's green.'**
Train your children from an early age.

**'If ye break yer legs,
don't come runnin' tae me.'**
If you are not going to take my advice
then don't ask me for help.

'Ye think aw yer eggs have twa yolks.'

You consider yourself as superior.

'Yer nose isnae a shoein' horn.'

Everything has a specific purpose.

'You could swing a monkey aff that petted lip.'

Don't take that attitude with me.

**'Stop sneezing. It's the wind
aff the devil's wings.'**

For goodness sake stop sneezing.

'Ah'm away fur the messages.'
I am away to do my shopping.

'This place is boggin'.'
The place is filthy.

'It's nearly twelve o'clock an' no an erse skelpt.'
I am behind with my domestic duties.

'Blaw that snottery nose.'
Your nose requires cleaning.

'Ye might no like it but ye'll thole it.'
You'll just need to get used to it.

'Och, it's jist fisslin'.'
It's just the wind whistling through the keyhole.

'It's aw mixie-maxy.'
Everything is confused.

'GOANAE NO DAE THAT!'

Food

'Ah'm fu', but ah'm no done.'
I've eaten my fill but I'm going to keep on eating.

'That wid gae ye a new mooth.'
That tastes extremely bitter.

'The maist accidents in life are served up.'
Some food that is provided is poor.

'Ah wid jist love a Chic Murray.'
I would like a curry.

'A horn spoon hauds nae poison.'
All the meals in this house are healthy.

'Better a sma' fish than an empty dish.'
Some food is better than no food.

'It's gey foostie.'

It has gone mouldy.

Happiness

'Pure dead brilliant!'
That's great.

**'They're no the happiest
that hae the maist gear.'**
Posessions don't necessarily bring happiness.

'Dinnae fash yersell.'
Do not worry.

**'Ye cannae buy peace o'
mind in the shops.'**
Having little to worry you is a blessing.

'GOANAE NO DAE THAT!'

'When sorrow sleeps,
dinnae wake it.'
Don't go over past concerns.

'East or west, hame is best!
There is no place like home.

'Some folks bring happiness alang
wherever they go. Ithers bring it
when they go!'
People bring happiness to others in
various ways.

'Happiness is a well-used doormat.'
Having friends will give you a happy life.

'Gae happiness awa but keep some fur yersell.'
Be kind to people but look after yourself, too.

'Yer jist as happy as ye think ye ur.'
A good frame of mind is essential to being content.

Health

'Ah'm pure done in.'
I'm exhausted.

'Nae room in that wan fur ony pain.'
They are thin.

'They shoes'll draw yer feet.'
That footware will make your feet sweat.

'Folks diet like sparrows then cannae stop chirpin' aboot it.'
The main topic of conversation for many people is their latest diet.

'GOANAE NO DAE THAT!'

'If yer the picture o' health
ye need a happy frame o' mind.'
People of a happy disposition tend to
keep well.

'Lang may yer lum reek,
an' may a wee moose never leave
yer kitchen press wi' a tear in its ee.'
May you live long and always have plenty to eat.

'Ye jist gae'd it a coo's lick.'
You only gave it one wipe
(usually their face or neck).

'Were ye lang bad efter ye took it?'
How long have you been ill?

'Yer lookin' awfa peely-wally.'
You are very pale.

'Whit whisky an' butter cannae
cure there's nae cure fur.'
An old 'cure'.

'Castor oil cures everythin'
but a widen leg.'
This medicine is good for you.

'That's the hair o' yer neck.'

That is the weak point in your make up.

'Yer a skinny malinkey lang legs.'

You are a tall and thin.

'Yer buttoned up the back like Achmahoy's dug.'

You are so thin I can see your spine.

'Oor doctor couldnae cure a plouk oan a coo's erse.'

The doctor I go to is not very good.

**'If ye step oan a crack in the pavement
yer faither wull get chilblains.'**

Come here and walk beside me.

'Ah've goat a stookie oan my arm.'

I have a plastercast on my arm.

'Only clean oot yer ear wi' yer elbow.'

Don't damage yourself
(especially by poking your finger in your ear).

**'Pull a hair oot an' seven ithers
will go tae its funeral.'**

Don't pull out any of your hair.

**'Ye don't wash yer dishcloot
an' yer knickers thegither.'**

Be sensible in life and in matters of health.

'Ah'm fair puckled.'

I am exhausted.

'An eatin' horse ne'er foundered.'

If you are eating well it is unlikely
that your end is near.

**'Muckle coo meat...
muckle maladies.'**

Too much meat can cause
health problems.

**'That yin could dae wi'
some loan-soup.'**

They need some milk straight
from the cow to improve their health.

Human Behaviour

'Pick a windae, yer leavin'.'
Get out!

'There's nought sae queer as folks.'
People are unpredictable.

'Yon has mere faces than the toon clock.'
They are not really to be trusted.

'She's a granny grey hips.'
She acts as though she's older than she is.

**'They that come wi' a crookit oxter
are welcome.'**
Someone who comes with a gift is welcome.

**'Dae ye think ah'm daft jist because
ah slaver at the mooth?'**
Don't try and con me.

**'Maist knockin' is done by folks who
dinnae know how tae ring the bell.'**
People who are incapable of doing what
you do will still criticise you.

'Butter doesnae stick tae yer breid.'
You are an unlucky person.

'A bald heid is soon shaven.'
Every situation has some advantage.

'Dinnae whistle if ye cannae sing.'
Don't bother wasting your time trying
to do something that you are obviously
incapable of doing.

**'Ah'm talkin' tae the shovel
no the dirt.'**
Aggressive statement which could
lead to confrontation.

'Some jist talk fae the mooth forward.'
Some people do not say what is truly on their mind

'The nod o' an honest man is enough.'
Honest people do not require contracts.

'It's no the size o' the dug in the ficht but the ficht in the dug.'
It is what is inside you that counts.

'Never blaw in a lug.'
Do not deceive people.

'Yer as greedy as ten cocks scrappin' a midden fur a barley pickle.'
You have a fantastic appetite.

'God sees maist things but neibers see aw things.'
Neighbours are mostly nosy.

'Gae's a wee keek.'
Let me have a look.

'Dinnae be a twa-legged creature wi' a goose's heid an' a hen's heart.'
Don't be a coward.

'Hae a guid whittle at yer belt.'
Always have a ready answer available.

'Yon's a right nippy-sweetie.'
They are sharp tongued.

'Some think they are nae sma drink.'
Some think they are better than they are.'

'Ye've a face like a torn melodeon.'
You look extremely upset.

**'Yer that far aheid o' yersel'
ye'll meet yersel' comin' back.**
Just live for today.

'That's pit yer gas at a peep.'
That has put you in your place.

'Bide a wee.'
Hold on for a bit.

'A helpin' haun helps twa.'

Helping someone can result in improving yourself.

'Mockin's catchin'.'

If you make a fool of someone you make
a fool of yourself.

'Gae's a wee shuftie.'

Let me have a look.

'Have a wee stoat doon.'

Wander down here.

'Ye cannae shove yer granny aff a bus.'
Grandparents are precious.

'A nod's as guid as a wink tae a blind horse.'
Here is a bit of information for you.

'Lock yer door an' keep the neighbours honest.'
Don't put temptation in anyone's road.

'Naethin' is got wi' delay but dirt an' lang nails.'
It does not pay to procrastinate.

The day hae eyes an' the nicht hae lugs.'
Someone always sees what you are doing.

'Eat peas wi' a prince an' cherries wi' a chapman.'
Treat everyone equally.

'Yon's crabbit.'
They are forever moaning.

'Keep the heid!'
Stay calm.

'Guilty consciences dinna need the polis.'
You know when you are in the wrong.

'He's guid at the jinkin'.'
He moves nimbly.

'It wis a bit of a kebbie-lebbie.'
Everyone was talking at the same time.

Insults

'Yer heid's mince.'
You seem confused.

'They're no' the full shilling.'
They are not too bright.

'Jist lies aboot like a lodging hoose cat.'
They do nothing but laze around.

'Away an' bile yer can!'
Get lost.

**'That wan couldna hit a coo
oan the backside wi' a banjo
even if they wur haudin' it by the tail.'**
They are absolutely useless.

**'You remind me o' a toothache
ah wance had.'**
You are a bit of a pain.

'Yon's a right chancer.'
He is not to be trusted.

'Not on yer bumbaleerie.'
No way will I do that.

'If it wis rainin' palaces you'd get hit wi' a dunnie door.'
You're a loser.

'Wur you haun-knitted?'
Are you daft?

'Yer as guid as ten men missin'.'
You are useless.

'Yon wid tak the skin aff yer custard.'
They are mean.

'Away an' wauchle.'
Get out of here.

'Whit an eedjit!'
They are daft.

'Away an' lie in the midden.'
Get lost!

'Ye couldna punch yer way oot a wet newspaper.'
You are pathetic.

'Yer as useless as a ten bob slider.'
You're as bad as old gym shoes.

'Gae it laldy!'
Let it rip.

'Ye wid marry a midden fur its muck!'
You have no standards.

'That yin's a right scunner.'
They are very irritating.

'Whit a bampot!'
They are an idiot.

'Yer talkin' mince withoot a tattie in sight.'
You are talking nonsense.

'Ya muckle gype.'
You are an idiot.

'Whit a numptie!'
He is a fool.

'Yer bum's oot the windae!'
You are talking rubbish.

'Away an' bile yer heid an' mak silly soup.'
Don't be silly.

'Yon's goat a brain like a tin o' corned beef.'
They are quite thick.

'Yer a half-melted welly.'
You are lacking in intelligence.

'Ye widnae look twice at that wee gomeril.'
He is an insignificant half-wit.

Self-Improvement

'Heid doon, erse up.'
Get busy.

'Ye'd mak a better door than a windae.'
You need to sharpen up.

'Guid claes an' keys get ye in.'
Dressing well can impress people.

**'Wink at sma' faults,
yer ain are muckle.'**

Do not be critical of others' faults
as you are not perfect.

**'Read auld books fae folks
lang awa.'**

Learn from the writings of wise
people of the past.

**'If ye don't like criticism,
say nothin', dae nothin'
and be nothin'.'**

Being criticised is part of life.

'Stop slitterin'.'
You are dripping food from
your mouth.

**'Dinnae clothe yer language
in rags.'**
Don't spoil what you say by including
bad language.

**'The best cure fur a short temper
is a lang walk.'**
You are better cooling off.

'Tarry Lang brought little hame.'
Do not waste time as you will achieve nothing.

**'Pick it up as the coo learned
the Heilin' fling.'**
Be self taught.

'A used key disnae rust.'
Keep educating yourself through life.

**'Yer future's a mirror wi'
broken glass.'**

You need to do something to
improve if you are going to get
on in life.

Love

'You're ma wee chookie hen.'
You are special to me.

**'If ye marry a chicken
ye'll get hen-pecked.'**
Watch who you marry.

'Love has wan e'e an' ower deef.'
Being in love means you ignore your
loved ones faults.

'Better half-hanged than ill-married.'

Don't marry until you are sure it is the right person.

'Mony a wifie shoulda stayed on her toes tae avoid a heel.'

Some people have unfortunately not married well.

'A fire that is oot is evil tae kindle.'

Don't start relationships with old flames.

'Beauty doesnae mak a man's purritch.'
There is more to selecting a wife than her looks.

'Some think nae man is guid enough
fur them. They may be richt or they
may be left.'
Some women are very fussy who they
wish for a mate.

'A bonny wife an' a back door
can mak a man poor.'
A pretty wife can still attract attention.

'That yin jist goes aroon
kissin' mirrors.'

The only person they love is
themselves.

'The moon disnae jist affect the tides,
ye know. It can stop caurs on dark roads.'

Romance and nature go hand in hand.

'Never marry a widow unless
her first husband wis hanged.'

Sometimes it is difficult to follow a caring
and loving first husband.

'It's nae use spilin'
twa hooses.'

Difficult people should just marry
each other rather than causing
problems in some other marriage.

Money

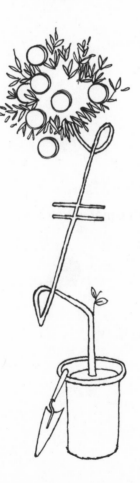

'Every penny's a prisoner.'
Don't be careless with your money.

'That yin's minted.'
They are well off.

'Mair than enough is ower muckle.'
Be content with the money you have.

'It's worth hee haw.'
It is worthless.

'If ah had your money ah wid burn ma ain.'
You are much better off than myself.

'Dae ye think Carnegie wis yer uncle?'
We are not rich.

'Ah've nae money but ma fether had piles.'
Our family is not well off. (Piles are haemorrhoids!)

'Dinnae stretch yer arm further than yer sleeve.'
Do not take on too much.

'There's mony a barber wid shave
a beardless man.'

When it comes to money be very careful.

'Dinnae waste a penny candle huntin'
fur a bawbee.'

Get your priorities right.

'Don't eat the calf in the coo's wame.'

Don't spend the money you have still to get.

'The money man's deid.'

I am skint.

'Guid steel is worth a penny.'
You have to pay for quality.

'Mony a mickle maks a muckle.'
Small savings mount up.

'A rich man has mair cousins than his fether had kin.'
Money attracts people.

'Cut yer coat tae suit yer pattern.'
Only spend what you can afford.

'Tis folly tae live poor an' die rich.'
Use your money wisely and enjoy living.

'He's a right bampot withoot
a silver sixpence tae his name.'
He is a silly, poor person.

'It's a lucky-measure.'
I am going to get more than I thought I would.

Philosophy

'It's a sair fecht fur jist half a loaf.'

No matter what you do you never totally
achieve your goals.

**'Gae some beggers a bed an'
they'll pay ye wi' a louse.'**

Some people take advantage of others.

**'Experience teaches fools, an'
fools willna learn nae ither way.'**

Many people only learn through bitter experience.

'Silent dugs also bite.'
Assume nothing.

'Dinnae eat cake tae save breid.'
Be sensible.

**'They that hae but wan ee maun
tend it weel.'**
If you have limited means then be
careful with it.

'Worry is like an auld rockin' chair.
It gaes ye somethin' tae dae but
doesnae get ye ony place.'

Try not to worry.

'Cracked bells ne'er mend.'

Get rid of items which will never
be of any use to you.

'Dinnae burn doon yer hoose
tae get rid o' the mice.'

Only take appropriate actions.

'It's as black as Willie's hatband an' tied nine times tae.'

It never ends.

'Dinnae expect somethin' new fae an echo.'

Be realistic in life.

'Three men can keep a secret if twa are deid.'

Keep your secrets to yourself.

'If ye feed the cat ye'll feed the mice.'
Think on the implications of your actions.

'Tae hang wi' poverty; pit anither pea in the soup.'
Let's spend a little more.

'Pit yer troubles in a pocket wi' a hole in it.'
Forget your problems.

**'The nicht is the mither o'
black thoughts.'**

Worries seem worse during the night.

**'A frein at court is worth a bob
or two in yer pocket.'**

Hang on to useful contacts.

'We're aw Jock Tamson's bairns.'

Everyone is equal.

**'Langest at the fireside,
soonest finds the cauld.'**

Individuals who are spoiled sometimes
find life difficult to cope with.

'Jump o'er rivers at the burn.'

Address your problems before they become big.

'Hittin' yer dug wi' a big stick is dead easy.'

You can always find an excuse for any action you take.

'Better tae say 'here it is' than 'here it wis'.'

Something you have is better than something gone.

'Back tae auld claes an' purridge.'
Back to the everyday pattern of life.

**'Dinnae buy anythin' fae a man pantin'
in the street.'**
Never buy from a doubtful source.

'Act daft an' get a free hurl.'
Let someone else do all the work.

**'A wise man doesnae hae his doctor
in his will.'**
Apply a bit of common sense.

'Shadows dinnae mak a noise.'
Always be on your guard.

'A dug wi twa owners is twice hungry.'
Make sure everyone knows what they are
responsible for.

'Whit's fur ye wull no go bye ye.'
What is meant to happen will happen.

'Castles fa' but wise words stey.'
Wisdom lasts.

'GOANAE NO DAE THAT!'

'God gave folks wan face but aw use anither.'
Most people do not reveal their true self.

'Dinnae pour water oan a drowned moose.'
Don't take unnecessary action.'

'If ye grasp the nettle mak sure there'
a docken leaf nearby.'
Always make sure you have a back-up plan.

'A blind man's wife needs nae painting.'
Don't do anything that is unnecessary.

'Ye cannae order Mrs Nature aboot.'

There is no way you can change the weather.

'Dinnae love ony strangers.'

Get to know people before you judge them.

'Truth isnae invented... only lies.'

It is better to tell the truth.

'Aw colours agree in the dark.'

We are all the same in darkness.

'It's a sair fecht fur half a loaf.'
It will take a lot of effort and achieve very little.

'The toon clock's stopped but it's right twice a day.'
Everything has its uses.

'Chase twa blackbirds an' catch nane.'
Get your priorities right.

'Aye, the day's no' yesterday.'
Every day brings its own issues.

Reputations

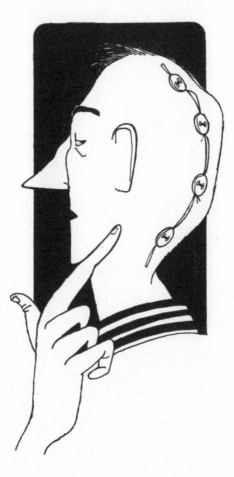

'It taks a lang spoon tae sup wi'
a fly Fifer.'

People from Fife are shrewd.

'Excuses are gie poor patches
oan the coat o' failure.'

Do a good job in the first place.

'The wan wi' the ladder's as bad
as the thief.'

Do not associate with bad people.

'They're the wee hen that never
laid away.'

They are not as innocent as they make out.

'They're gonnae meet themselves
cummin' back.'

They are very clever.

'Dae ye think ma heid buttons
up the back?'

Do you think I am a fool?

**'If black's yer apron,
ye'll aye be washin' it.'**

It is difficult to change a bad reputation.

'Guid folks hae costly names.'

Good reputations are hard earned.

**'The deil's bairns hae aye their
daddy's luck.'**

Rogues seem to have a bit of luck.

'Yon thinks they are nae sma' drink.'
They think they are something special.

'She's aye a wee bit harty.'
She is fussy and somewhat frugal.

'She likes wee dabbie-douces.'
She has a hankering for small, fancy items.

Work

'Yons intae everything but a workin' jaikit.'

They are lazy and workshy.

'There's mair tae ploughin' than whistlin'.'

Don't assume everything is easy.

'Footprints in the sands o' time urnae made by sittin' doon.'

If you wish to leave your mark you must work hard.

'Ma jaiket is oan a shoogly nail.'
I am unsure of long-term employment.

'Measure twice, cut wance.'
Double check your decision before
going ahead.

**'Barrows only move when ye
gae them a shove.'**
You have to act and not just talk.

'He's goat paralysis o' the galluses.'
He's a lazy lump.

'The day efter the morn it'll
be the middle o' the week,
an ye huvnae done a haun's
turn yet.'
Get a move on with your work.

'He that wid thrive must rise by five;
he that has thriven may lie tae seven.'
The sooner you do this job the sooner
you will get a rest.

'Ye cannae plough the field jist
by turnin' it ow'r in yer mind.'

Do more than just think about doing something.

'Yer as guid as an aspidistra oan
a wally pedestral.'

You just seem to stand around and do nothing.

'He jist got his jotters.'

He has been dismissed from his job.

'The tatties are over the side.'

You've made a poor job of this.

'Naebuddy ever drooned in their
ain sweat.'

Work harder.

'Tae eat the fruit first climb the tree.'

You have to work to achieve your goals.

'Find a job ye like an' ye'll ne'er hae
tae work a day in yer life.'

If you enjoy your job you will not look
on it as hard work.

'Guid work tastes sweet.'

You get satisfaction from a job well done.

Some other books published by **LUATH** PRESS

Haud ma Chips, Ah've Drapped the Wean! Glesca Grannies' Sayings, Patter and Advice

Allan Morrison,
illustrated by Bob Dewar
ISBN 978 1 908373 47 2 PBK £7.99

 In yer face, cheeky, kindly, gallus, astute; that's a Glesca granny for you. Glesca grannies' communication is direct, warm, expressive, rich and often hilarious.

'Dinnae cross yer eyes. Ye'll end up like that squinty bridge.'

'Oor doctor couldnae cure a plouk oan a coo's erse.'

'This is me since yesterday.'

'That wan wid breastfeed her weans through the school railings.'

'Yer hair looks like straw hingin' oot a midden.'

'Ah'm jist twenty-wan an' ah wis born in nineteen-canteen.'

'The secret o' life is an aspirin a day, a wee dram, an' nae sex oan Sundays.'

Glesca grannies shoot from the mouth and get right to the point with their sayings, patter and advice. This book is your guide to the infallible wisdom of the Glesca granny.

Should've Gone to Specsavers, Ref! The Trials and Tribulations of Big Erchie Smith

Allan Morrison,
illustrated by Bob Dewar
ISBN 978 1 908373 73 1 PBK £7.99

 The referee. You can't have a game without one. The most hated man (or woman) in football but you have to invite one to every game.

Enjoy a laugh at the antics and wicked humour of Scottish referee Big Erchie, a powerhouse at five foot five, and a top grade referee who strikes fear into he hearts of managers and players alike as he stringently applies the laws of the game.

But Big Erchie is burdened with a terrible secret... He's a Partick Thistle supporter.

Last Tram Tae Auchenshuggle: Have a final shoogle with Glasgow's famous clippie Big Aggie MacDonald

Allan Morrison,
illustrated by Mitch Miller
ISBN 978 1 908373 04 5 PBK £7.99

'Wur full! Everybuddy haud ontae a strap or yer man!'

It's the end of the line for Glasgow's famous clippie, Big Aggie MacDonald, as her beloved trams are destined for the big depot in the sky.

Last Tram tae Auchenshuggle! is a trip down memory lane to 1962, with the Glasgow tram service about to come to an end. But Aggie wants to enjoy the last months on her beloved caurs, dishing out advice and patter with her razorsharp wit to the unwary: the outspoken clippie who was never outspoken!

Big Aggie's tram is pure theatre, and the clippie is something else when it comes to dealing with fare dodgers, drunks, wee nyaffs, cheeky weans and highfalutin' wummen.

'Get aff! O-f-f, aff! Dae ye no' understaun' the Queen's English?'

If History was Scottish

Norman Fergusson
ISBN 978 1 908373 67 0 PBK £7.99

An alternative look at notable figures and events as seen through a unique Caledonian perspective. The attributes associated with being Scottish are applied to well-known quotes and events. Covering topics such as war, politics, cinema, religion and more, the text will be accompanied by light-hearted and witty illustrations making this an ideal book for the gift market both in Scotland and further afield.

Dae ye Ken?

Vicki Gausden
ISBN 978 1 905222 59 9 PBK £5.99

 This work is split thematically and includes subjects from clothes (claes) to feelings through food and drink, socialising (gang oot on the toon) and that favourite Scottish topic – the weather. *Dae Ye Ken?* is an illustrated mini Scots/English thesaurus. Fully approved by experts at the Scots Language Resource Centre.

Scots We Ken

Julie Davidson,
illustrated by Bob Dewar
ISBN 978 1 906307 00 4 HBK £9.99

 Natives know them. Visitors soon get to know them. Some, like the Golf Club Captain, the Last Publican and the Nippy Sweetie, are endangered species; others, like the Whisky Bore and the Munrobagger, are enduring figures on the Scottish landscape. Every generation produces its own variations on the Scottish character and it doesn't take long for the newcomers to become familiar social types like the MSP, the Yooni Yah, the Rural Commuter and the Celebrity Chieftain. Most Scots, if they're honest, will recognise a little bit of themselves in one or other of thes mischievous and frighteningly accurate portraits. Julie Davidson's wickedly observed profiles are complemented by Bob Dewar's witty drawings in this roguish gallery of 'Scots We Ken'.

Details of these and other books published by Luath Press can be found at: **www.luath.co.uk**

Luath Press Limited

committed to publishing well written books worth reading

LUATH PRESS takes its name from Robert Burns, whose little collie Luath (*Gael.*, swift or nimble) tripped up Jean Armour at a wedding and gave him the chance to speak to the woman who was to be his wife and the abiding love of his life. Burns called one of 'The Twa Dogs' Luath after Cuchullin's hunting dog in Ossian's *Fingal*. Luath Press was established in 1981 in the heart of Burns country, and now resides a few steps up the road from Burns' first lodgings on Edinburgh's Royal Mile. Luath offers you distinctive writing with a hint of unexpected pleasures.

Most bookshops in the UK, the US, Canada, Australia, New Zealand and parts of Europe either carry our books in stock or can order them for you. To order direct from us, please send a £sterling cheque, postal order, international money order or your credit card details (number, address of cardholder and expiry date) to us at the address below. Please add post and packing as follows: UK – £1.00 per delivery address; overseas surface mail – £2.50 per delivery address; overseas airmail – £3.50 for the first book to each delivery address, plus £1.00 for each additional book by airmail to the same address. If your order is a gift, we will happily enclose your card or message at no extra charge.

Luath Press Limited
543/2 Castlehill
The Royal Mile
Edinburgh EH1 2ND
Scotland

Telephone: 0131 225 4326 (24 hours)
email: sales@luath.co.uk
Website: www.luath.co.uk